Also illustrated by Patricia MacCarthy and published by Dent,
Seventeen Kings and Forty-two Elephants by Margaret Mahy

First published in 1989
© Patricia MacCarthy 1989
All rights reserved
Printed in Italy
for J.M. Dent & Sons Ltd
91 Clapham High Street, London SW4

British Library Cataloguing in Publication Data
  Animals galore.
  1. English language. Readers. For pre-school
  children
  I. Title
  428.6

  ISBN 0-460-07034-7

Animals Galore!

Patricia MacCarthy

J.M. DENT & SONS LTD
London

a pride of lions

a herd of elephants

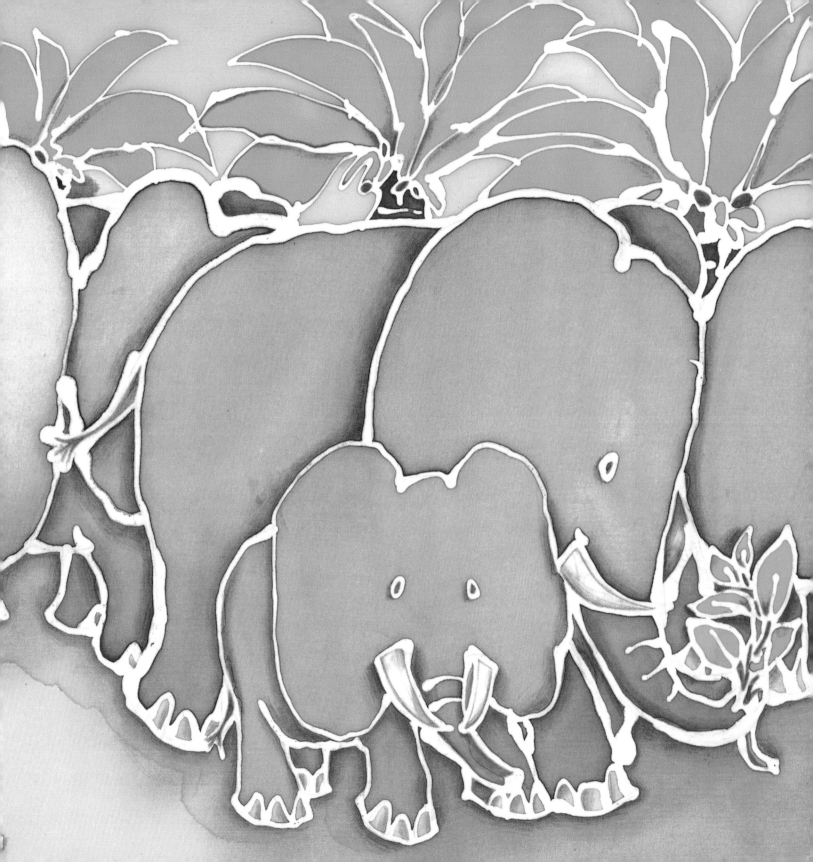

a colony of penguins

a shoal of fish

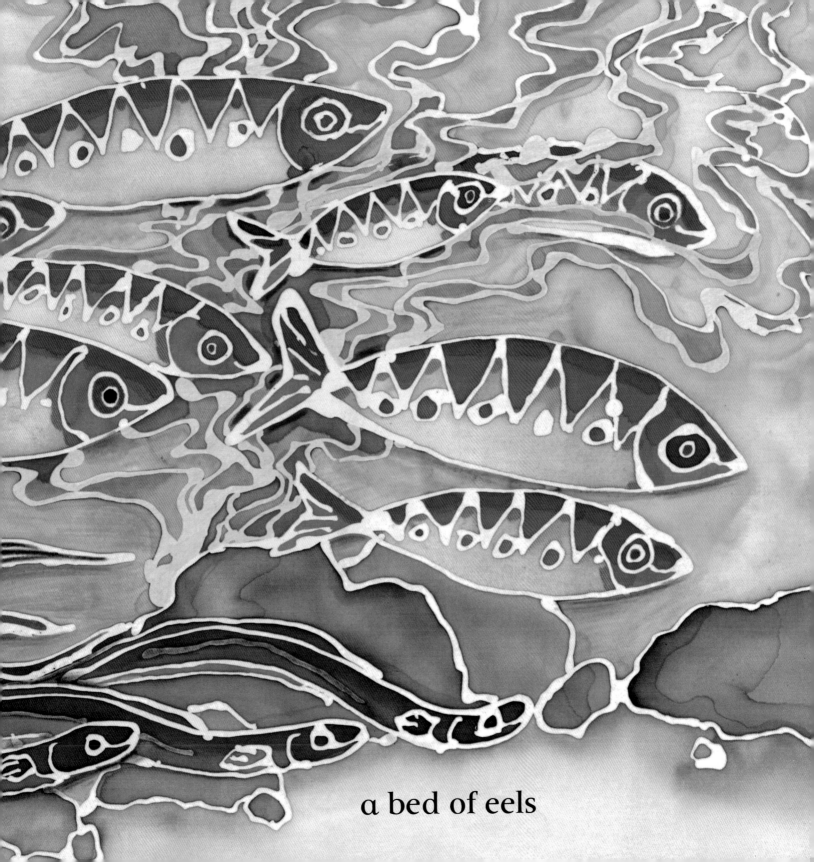

a bed of eels

a pack of wolves

a school of dolphins

a knot of toads

a swarm of bees

an army of ants

a drove of buffalo

a murder of crows

a clouder of cats

a horde of gnats

a company of parrots

a troop of monkeys

a gaggle of geese

a flock of sheep

a litter of piglets

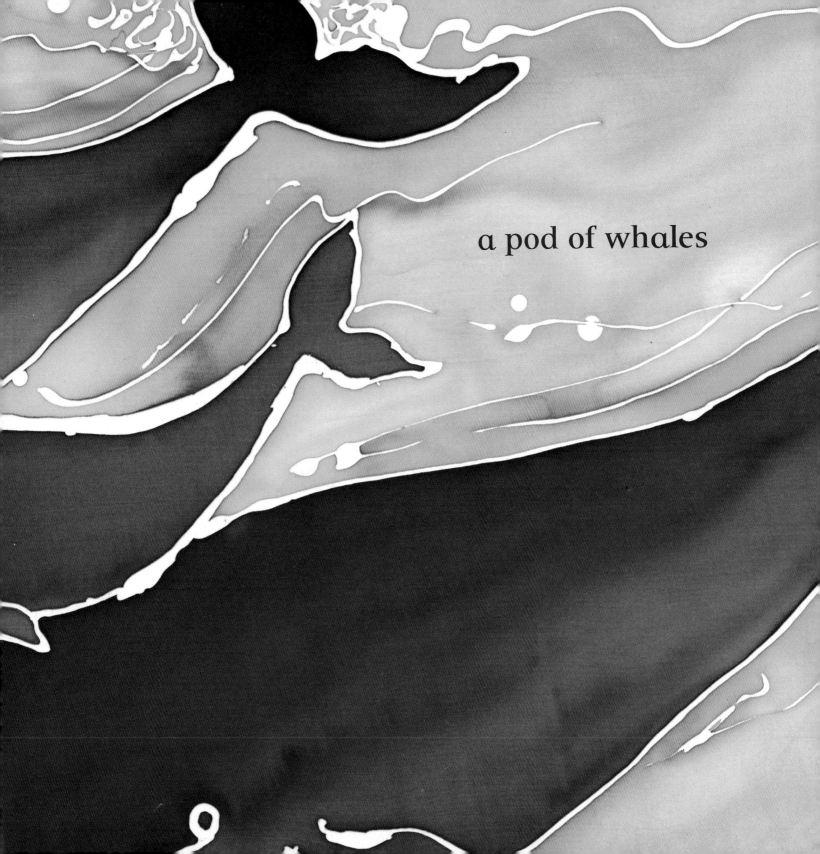

a pod of whales

DUE DATE

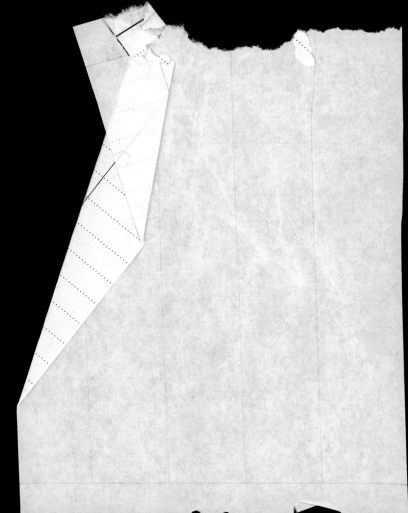

28-8-91

BRUSS